AMOUR-PROPRE

AFFIRMING LOVE FOR ONE'S SELF

RAVI VERMA

ISBN 978-1-68586-271-8

"Dedicated to my self."

Contents

Contents

Acknowledgements

Special thanks
to my lovely sister Eno and
my dearest mother for helping me
out in creating the illustrations
present in this mini book.
Love you both
so much!

Preface

Amour-propre are two french words written in a way that literally means "self-love".

It is the first book in the series Unconditional. Unconditional aims to share the author's approach and understanding of love: its presence, value, different forms, etc.

This book hides inside the sentiments of affection we should have for our 'self'. Remembering how far we have come and showing gratitude for the state of well-being and content life has helped us to enjoy after each hurdle we passed.

The ups and downs in life teach many things necessary, including the most important one => "self-love".

The poems in this book encourage mainly to recognize the importance of self-love, self-worth, acceptance, etc. Some of them talk about the negative effects a wrong choice may cause and warn for the same. Some may sound sarcastic, some may trigger hope, and some are likely to motivate you to take needed actions towards self's betterment.

PREFACE

The entire motive of this book is to share the importance of self-love as said earlier because when we start loving our 'self', we then try to create a positive environment around us that only focuses and works towards upliftment(all-inclusive).

Ravi Verma
15.04.2021

Let's Begin The Journey Of Self-love

accept reality

honour the disparate

respect the existence

trust the essence

cherish the good

allow to embrace

acknowledge the inner voice

have faith in I

Affirmation #1

Stop Demeaning Comparisons

I am present in this universe to celebrate and be proud of my uniqueness.

1. It Troubles

I hear them giggle at first,
turn their backs,
then burst laughter.
Pointing pupils wherever I go,
sadist minds with diffident souls.
Chuckles hiding terrible lives,
miserable self mocks else's lives.

2. Censorious Mind

Covered mirrors were ageing fast,
shiny smooth surface didn't last.
Bland in white,
impure in black.
Reflection too critical,
torturous and cynical.
Even a glance for a chance,
deterred from the entrance.
Full of doubts and diffidence,
persona shedding tears of hesitance.
All vanished with just a praise,
seemed very foreign those words full of grace.
A streak that grew larger,
shredding fibers of the outer cover.
Portraying truth with glistening glamour,
exuberant aura cheering further.

Affirmation #2

Opinions Are Just Opinions

I, being the one who experienced, took action, dealt, and survived the situation, own the absolute right over the narration as per my discretion.

3. It Affects

Shady remarks seem to overpower,
gloomy thoughts flaunt their power.
Overwhelming flow of murky tides,
in a compact corner radiance hides.
Self-doubt weakens intellectual link,
impotent body jumps off the brink.

4. Believe Or Not

You seem to be a very nice soul,
but there's many tales of you being foul.
I wonder why your character has been torn,
among the groups of wise you are compared with a thorn.
They give you the side-eye as you keep walking on your lane,
trying to misconstrue and put down anything you leave behind
on your trail.
I wonder how they then scream for justice for their own,
while still being judgmental on the fact that you chose to live
alone.
Are those just assumptions, they share to water their own thirst?
maybe their scalded sadist land finds relief when someone breaks
your trust.
I am sure they grin from ear to ear, clink cheers then wait for
more,
celebrate your misery, shush their ego,
mourn over their reality, fogged behind mapped travesty.

Affirmation #3

Mistakes Prove Attempts

I may still be searching for my purpose as a human being but I
need to believe that work in progress is better than a halted work.

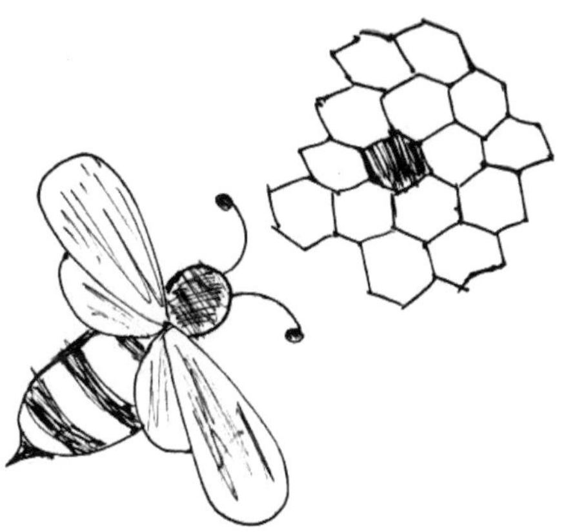

5. Efforts

How much more would this bother you?
this failure is just one of few.
A ride to the top has to end somewhere,
before it starts to descend, use that time to prepare.
Each turn has a new lesson,
that keeps fueling the flames of ambition.
What you need is the courage to try,
even for once, at least strive a trial.
Never worry for what's unknown,
predictions and probabilities aren't certain.

6. Progress

There's a definite end for every tale,
but what stays strong after, is the supple morale.
Ready to be perceived in any fashion,
as long as it prompts an enthusiastic action.
Inspiration helps feed aspiration,
procuring, watering the seeds of progression.
Do not be afraid or let the determination spoil,
drag yourself through each challenging turmoil.
Progress is a continuous process,
towards failure or triumph, all upon your decisiveness.

Affirmation #4

My Psyche is Valuable Than The Body Itself

I prioritize being loving, kind, friendly, and understanding more than the exterior attractiveness.

7. Enough No More

An incessant journey of upgrading roles,
tackling new horrors while reaching for goals.
Achievements now tiring the spirit, mind, body, and soul,
abundance feels unfulfilling to the core.
Why do I think I want more?
I really don't feel the need to gain furthermore.
I keep losing peace while gaining more,
commotion strangulates my quietude ore.

8. It Ain't Worth

Weary, dreary, teary days,
jostling for more, using terrible ways.
The search for better continues,
quenched cravings reawakens.
Impatient actions cause too much load,
vulnerable soul left exposed.
It ain't worth, do realise,
choose peace and love both, don't partite.
Stillness blooms open wide,
only relaxed spirit shares serene vibe.

Affirmation #5

Let Toxicity Go

I am determined to keep my soul pure and unaffected by the negative and ignorant vibe of others.

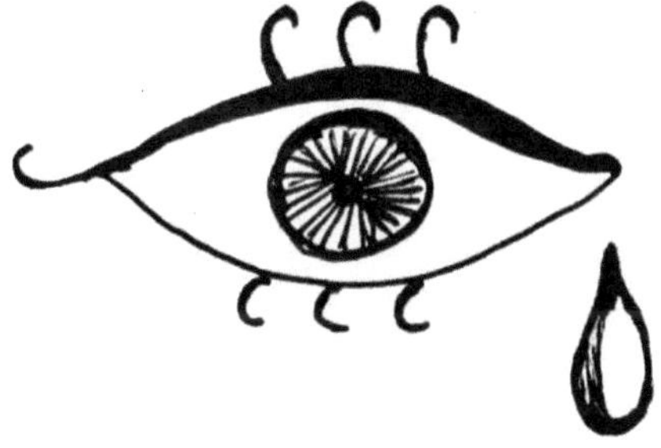

9. Escape

Escape, don't stay,
try to find a gateway.
You don't deserve toxicity,
why live accordingly.
Stop wearing the cover of anonimity,
you too have dreams and individuality.
Do not feel stuck,
you can bet your luck.
Believe me,
it's okay to flee.
You have been groomed this way,
sculpted over time to make you stay.
Every carving done to seal your will,
forced dependence over necessary bills.
Ensuring no motion,
numb emotions.
In a shabby museum you are kept,
bombarded with the excuses of a possible theft.
Distanced from others,
all helpful figures.
Use your own intuition,
avoid this situation.

10. Addiction

A rush infatuating senses,
oozing charm, muddling awareness.
Excited body,
celebrating breifly.
A long unconscious silence,
pain persuading intellect's absence.
Surfacing impulse feels irresistible,
a slight sensation of the actuality, causes courage to tremble.
Intentions and thoughts surge,
choice to be made, either avoid or indulge.
Wisdom impedes unwanted resonance,
knowing it's easier to drift and loose the balance.
Surround self amidst fellow allies,
be thoughtful, it is never late to realise.

Affirmation #6

Leave Unwanted Baggage

I believe in moving forward and not burdening myself with guilt for a long period of time.

11. Pursue

Break irrational barriers,
hear your heart's faint screams.
Disparaging your desires,
wouldn't discourage the upcoming dreams.
Help yourself, please,
your own worth is at stake, don't leave.
time is signalling you to take the responsibility,
make choices that support your true fantasy.

12. Tears

Outburst necessary for relief,
therapeutic as per my belief.
Amazing how it refreshes and replenishes,
saturates the spirit with newness.
Every drop that abandons eyes,
evacuates with part of the sadness.
Strong-minds don't mind to show,
what's held inside needs to flow.

Affirmation #7

I Can Trust My Self

I am the only one who wants, needs, and is willing to work for the happiness of myself.

13. Seeking Validity

You are already approved by god,
awarded with such an elaborate bod.
Gifted with life to fulfil meaningful purposes,
breathing every breath with a determination for success.
You do not need any validity,
you have been affirmed by the supreme holy.
Do not seek for any validations from others,
choice if bad remains unchanged even if in large numbers.
You know what's better for your own wellness,
you grew gaining experience to deal with these circumstances.

14. Innately Strong

Consciousness overwhelmed with undesirable questions,
a moment of disbalance aware mind experiences.
Strong-willed psyche in control,
proved itself resilient by balancing all.
We are innately intuitive,
senses sensing proofless alternative.
Trust more on your instinctive core,
you'll regret less and be at peace more.

Affirmation #8

My Emotions & Feelings Matter

I prioritize myself and that is not selfish in any way as it inevitably helps me to then care for others and share love.

15. I Matter

So many gifts you own,
yet so many times you feel alone.
You wander seeking facade affirmations,
mining for compliments and validations.
Willing to degrade your moral foundation,
chasing momentary applause and recognition.
Unaware of the internal injuries this causes,
you carry on with the reckless manoeuvres.
Stop these actions and pay attention,
you too need care, respect, love, and affection.
Like all other beings you are hungry for support,
stop wandering around aimlessly in search of comfort.
Try being the one who praises self,
acknowledging your qualities and being grateful for this life.
Grow faith and credence in I,
I is faithful enough to always reside by your side.

16. Agreement

You don't have to agree everytime,
for everything or with everyone.
You can discern your choice,
assist your opinions by granting your voice.
Don't make an agreement with the speculated lies,
you define yourself, bearing the truth of your lows and highs.
Don't expect acceptation from others,
it's not them, it's your self who really cares.
when you own your own,
you no more care for the unworthy unknown.

Affirmation #9

I Fill The Half-Empty Glass With Optimism

I have learned that there's nothing wrong with seeking more while not losing peace of mind. What I have is enough for now.

17. Higher Energy

I believe in the existence of higher energy,
the energy behind life's prophecy.
Plethora of life keeps adding more members,
all need to commit for establishing standards.
I am blessed enough to maintain stability,
have faith that shares sense of security.
I'll keep working on my fears and anxiety,
cherishing life while promoting humanity.

18. Good

Spring of hope finally arrived,
the acts of good have greatly spiked.
An appealing scent swayed me,
overwhelming my core with joy and glee.
Alluring with the aroma of qualities,
positive percipience spreads, attracting swarms of bees.
My belief in goodness has again bloomed,
I now no more have the feeling of being doomed.

Affirmation #10

I Am Kind To Myself

I am the very first one to celebrate my accomplishments and give enormous compliments.

19. Warmth

Just a smile and a nod,
nothing more, I demand.
Kind gestures,
tender actions.
Friendly behavior,
compassionate character.
Filled with love,
I feel sad no more.
Enthusiasm rises tall,
sharing warmth with all.

20. Let's Meditate

Relax,
take deep breaths.
Close your eyes,
wipe out negative vibes.
Enjoy this emptiness
serene mindfulness,
Now, imagine yourself standing in front of a door,
entering which you step on a feathery cloudy floor.
As the mist around clears dramatically,
you find yourself amidst a garden so heavenly.
With flora and fauna abundant,
magical creatures of your dreams being present.
Pleasant scenery effaces emotional burden,
You enjoy cuddling, soaking in warm affection.
stay there for a while,
while embracing peace.
Say farewells and leave with a promise,
vowing to visit the place on a regular basis.
Before leaving, do close the door,
open your eyes and continue with your regular chore.

The Journey Should Never End

doubt the doubt that doubts your worth
useless and futile is that doubt, not thou
pivot on self
rescue lost respect
reap the good
archive the hurt
protect your peace
armour all round health

About The Author

Ravi Verma is an Indian Writer. Born and brought up among Indian Tibetan society as his father Dr. Kanta Prasad Verma was posted as a Teacher in Central School for Tibetans which is an educational institution working as a step to help Tibetan refugees by educating them and helping to conserve their identity, culture, and tradition. He is a Nature lover, and most of his poems are based on Nature and the need for an optimistic and kind attitude towards every living being, which is must for this generation and era full of hopelessness, cruelty, and pessimism.

Write & Share

Meditate for a while and then write down three things that you learnt from this book or five things that you already knew. You can take a picture and share your answer with me. I'll be happy to read your take-away.

Crossword For Good

Search for words in the crossword and write sentences using them on the next page that you think served or will serve for your journey of self-love. I would love to get to know how you used the words, you can share them with me through any of the social media platform.

<table>
<tr><td>T</td><td>R</td><td>U</td><td>S</td><td>T</td><td>G</td><td>P</td><td>W</td></tr>
<tr><td>E</td><td>G</td><td>O</td><td>D</td><td>R</td><td>R</td><td>U</td><td>O</td></tr>
<tr><td>A</td><td>M</td><td>A</td><td>L</td><td>U</td><td>A</td><td>R</td><td>R</td></tr>
<tr><td>M</td><td>A</td><td>B</td><td>A</td><td>O</td><td>A</td><td>S</td><td>T</td></tr>
<tr><td>D</td><td>E</td><td>A</td><td>R</td><td>M</td><td>V</td><td>U</td><td>H</td></tr>
<tr><td>N</td><td>I</td><td>C</td><td>E</td><td>A</td><td>Y</td><td>E</td><td>A</td></tr>
<tr><td>I</td><td>G</td><td>O</td><td>O</td><td>D</td><td>C</td><td>F</td><td>E</td></tr>
<tr><td>K</td><td>S</td><td>E</td><td>L</td><td>F</td><td>Z</td><td>E</td><td>S</td></tr>
</table>

A Note Expressing Gratitude

"Thank you so much for investing your time and reading this book. I hope this book helped you gain something good that can help ignite love and positivity within you. Wish you the best for your present and future endeavors. Thank you once again. Would love to hear/read your thoughts on the book and connect with you."

Would love to connect with you on:

Instagram: **@ravivermawriter**

Twitter: **@ravivermawriter**

Facebook: **@writerraviverma**

Printed by Libri Plureos GmbH in Hamburg,
Germany